Spiritual Warfare

Fighting the Good Fight

by Vivian Boland OP

*All booklets are published thanks to the
generous support of the members of the
Catholic Truth Society*

CATHOLIC TRUTH SOCIETY
PUBLISHERS TO THE HOLY SEE

Contents

Introduction

In 1589 an Italian priest, Lorenzo Scupoli (1530-1610), published a book called *Spiritual Combat*. In less than twelve months it was being used by St Francis de Sales, then a young student at Padua. Referring to it as his spiritual director, Francis treasured this book all his life, reading a passage every day and the whole book every month. Quickly translated into many languages, it joined Thomas à Kempis' *Imitation of Christ* as one of the classic manuals of Catholic spirituality. Its success came from its simplicity, its practical character, and the way in which its teaching rang true, forged as it was in the crucible of Fr Scupoli's personal suffering. John Henry Newman (1801-1890) used it, especially in the years of his conversion, and it helped form the spiritual life of Blessed John XXIII (1881-1963) when he was a young seminarian at Bergamo. Nicodemos the Hagiorite (1748-1809), one of the editors of the *Philokalia*, the standard collection of spiritual writings of Eastern Orthodoxy, adapted it for Orthodox Christians.

In recent years Scupoli's work is not so well known, perhaps because the themes of self-denial, self-distrust, and even doing violence to oneself in order to follow

Christ, trouble rather than encourage people. But any serious spiritual teaching involves discipline and the practice of asceticism, a readiness to engage in the struggle with oneself, with the powers of the spiritual world, and with the mystery of how we come to prefer God's will to our own. In each of the gospels Jesus teaches that those who want to follow him must deny themselves and take up their cross, and that those who lose their life for his sake will find it (*Mt* 16:24-25; *Mk* 8:34-35; *Lk* 9:23-24; *Jn* 12:25).

In 1943 a French Jesuit, Henri de Lubac, wrote an essay called *Spiritual Warfare*. In this work the future Cardinal identifies the attack on it by the German philosopher Friedrich Nietzsche as the greatest contemporary challenge facing Christianity. For de Lubac this challenge was not just a political and philosophical one although it was that for sure - he writes in a France occupied and partitioned by the Nazis - it is also a spiritual and theological challenge. 'The Christian who wants to remain faithful', he writes, 'can only reject with a categorical *No* a neopaganism that is constituted against Christ' (page 500).

The warfare in which the Christian must engage is on many levels, then, not just the personal moral and spiritual quest but also the social intellectual and political contest, what has more recently come to be called 'the culture war'. It is worth noting that when used correctly the Arabic term 'jihad' has a similar range of meanings as Christians give to the 'spiritual warfare'. The so-called 'Greater Jihad' refers to the personal spiritual struggle to be ever more faithful to God.

The language of combat and warfare is not fashionable in spirituality or theology today. It is clearly open to misunderstanding and abuse. Yet there are many places in the New Testament where the Christian life is presented in just these terms, as warfare (2 *Co* 10:4), struggle (*Ph* 1:30; *Col* 1:29; *Heb* 10:32; 12:4), a fight (1 *Tm* 1:18), an athletic contest or *agonia* (1 *Co* 9:24), a boxing-match with oneself (1 *Co* 9:27), a readiness to kill things in ourselves and in our relationships (*Rm* 8:13), a conflict between good and evil (*Jn* 5:29; *Rm* 7:21), light and darkness (*Lk* 11:34-36; *Jn* 3:19), truth and falsehood (*Jn* 8:44), life and death (*Rm* 6:13,23). In this conflict we are participants and not just spectators, agents but also victims dependent on the power of Christ if we are to survive it. In 1996 John Paul II wrote that spiritual combat is 'a demanding reality which is not always given due attention today' (*Vita consecrata* § 38).

At the moment in which a person asks to be admitted to the Church as a catechumen he or she is asked to reject 'every power which sets itself up in opposition to God and his Christ' as well as 'every form of worship which does not offer God true honour'. Soon after this the catechumen receives the exorcisms and is reminded that the spiritual life is a battle between flesh and spirit, that self-denial is needed if we are to gain the blessings of the Kingdom of God, and that God's help is needed continually. The prayers of exorcism refer to evil spirits, to falsehood and sin, to all forms of immorality, to the tyranny of the enemy, to the spirit of falsehood, greed and wickedness, to the spirit of selfishness and greed, of pleasure and worldly pride. The person is then anointed with the oil of catechumens, an athlete's oil to strengthen them for the contest. Baptism is the beginning of a struggle, more or less severe according to God's providence, that ends only at the moment of death.

This booklet does not pretend to emulate either Scupoli or de Lubac. All that is attempted is a survey of the theme of spiritual warfare in the Bible. This is done in four parts: the struggle with ourselves, with powers that are 'not just flesh and blood', and with God, and a reflection on how these aspects of Christian spiritual warfare are embraced and resolved in the work of Jesus Christ, our leader and victorious champion.

The Struggle
with Ourselves

A Threefold Temptation

In its account of the original sin, the Book of Genesis tells us that the human beings decided to take the fruit for three reasons:

- because it was good to eat
- because it was pleasing to the eye
- because they judged it desirable for the knowledge it could give.

These phrases from Genesis 3:6 are echoed towards the end of the Bible in the First Letter of Saint John. All that is in the world, it says,

- the lust of the flesh
- the lust of the eyes
- the pride of life

is not of the Father but is of the world (1 *Jn* 2:16). These are the attractions of transgression, the factors that make sin possible.

The Bible seems to offer us a threefold pattern of temptation, then, and not just in these two texts. The temptations of Jesus can be interpreted according to this pattern (*Mt* 4:1-11; *Mk* 1:12-13; *Lk* 4:1-13). One is about feeding his hunger, a lust of the flesh. Another is about displaying his power, a lust of the eyes, something to impress. And the third is about taking on God, putting God's wisdom to the test, and standing over against God somehow, being as wise as, even wiser than, God.

The Book of Deuteronomy speaks of the paths to sin as

- a straying heart
- surrender to idolatry
- a refusal to listen (*Dt* 30:15-20)

and the Book of Sirach warns us against

- following passion
- giving our hearts to money
- saying 'I am self-sufficient, who has authority over me' (*Si* 5:1-8).

It seems, that this threefold pattern does structure the universal human experience of temptation. What touches us deeply attracts us powerfully,

- firstly the desires and needs of the body
- secondly what is pleasing and delightful whether in our own eyes or in the eyes of others

- thirdly the desire for knowledge and the power and autonomy it brings.

What tempts the human being are the satisfaction of bodily needs, perhaps to the point of indulgence; having some standing in the world through the things one possesses that are admired by others; and taking control of one's life, becoming wise in one's own estimation, to the point of not needing anybody else, even God. There is much to be gained from meditating on this threefold pattern.

The Christian Triangle

Another way of thinking about this is to say that the temptations that come our way will inevitably concern

- relating to self
- relating to others
- relating to God.

If we think of these as the three corners of a triangle, then we can say that it is within this triangle that the Christian is called to live, remembering always God, others and self. If we remember one of these to the exclusion of the other two, or we remember two to the exclusion of the third, then we are not remembering all that needs to be thought about as we reflect on our following of Christ.

Spiritual warfare, the struggle against sin and temptation, involves battles at each corner of this triangle, sometimes in relation to oneself, sometimes in relation to the challenges posed to us by others and our dealings with them, sometimes with regard to God. The Christian tradition has fixed on seven deadly sins, pride, covetousness, lust, anger, gluttony, envy and sloth. Each of these attacks one or more corners of this triangle, our relationship with God, with others, or with ourselves. The major spiritual battles in which we find ourselves engaged, whichever deadly sin they are about, involve all three corners of the triangle. No aspect of Christian life is adequately considered without constantly remembering all three. The great commandment that summarises the duties of the Christian life makes this clear:

> You shall love **the Lord your God** with all your heart, and with all your soul, and all your mind. This is the great and first commandment. And a second is like it, You shall love your **neighbour** as **yourself** (*Mt* 22:37-39).

Any aspect of Christian life - say reconciliation and forgiveness - cannot be established if we neglect any corner of the Christian triangle. When they think about forgiveness and reconciliation people tend to think first of their relationship with others. But difficulties experienced in that corner of the triangle might well find at least part of their explanation in one of the other corners, for example in the fact that there are ways in which people cannot forgive themselves, or even that there are things about which they cannot forgive God. Inability to forgive ourselves gets in the way of our ability to forgive others. Lorenzo Scupoli is realistic and encouraging in telling us that we will sin, so the thing to do is simply acknowledge our failure, ask forgiveness and help from God, and get on with things.

Inability to forgive God is more complex. If it is accepted that we might on occasion be angry with God, then it seems acceptable also to think that there might be ways in which we find it difficult to forgive God. For what might we need to forgive God? Well, for being God when we are not, or for having His own will about our lives and for not revealing it more clearly to us (for so it seems to us most of the time). To say that there is no way in which I need to be reconciled not only *with* God but *to* God is to say that I understand his wisdom completely and that there is no room for the garden of Gethsemane in my relationship with God.

When we reflect on temptation and its roots we quickly find ourselves recognising this triangle. To reflect adequately on living the Christian life I need to think not only about myself and others but also about God, not only about myself and God but also about others, not only about others and God but also about myself.

The Weapons of this Warfare

The threefold asceticism of Lent, which is the threefold asceticism of the Christian life at any time, consists of almsgiving, prayer and fasting (*Mt* 6:1-18). Notice that the three corners of the Christian triangle are addressed in these practices

- almsgiving concerns others
- prayer concerns God
- fasting concerns myself.

Notice that we can also align these practices with the threefold structure of temptation identified earlier. The attractions of transgression are the lust of the flesh, the lust of the eyes and the pride of life (1 *Jn* 2:16), what is good to eat, pleasing to the eye and promises wisdom (*Gn* 3:6). These things are not in themselves our enemies but they are the things that most easily turn against us when we pursue them disproportionately.

How are the classical ascetical practices the antidote to temptation?

- fasting and other disciplines of self-denial help us to manage the desires of the flesh in ways that are appropriate to our true needs as well as to our commitments and relationships

- almsgiving and other practices of charity and justice-making help us to manage our relationships with others, our standing in the world and our evaluation of what is important in regard to possessions, reputation and achievement

- prayer and other acts of the virtue of religion - adoration, devotion and sacrifice - sustain our relationship with God and help us appreciate that it is in God we live and move and have our being (*Ac* 17:28).

There is a tendency now to value human beings simply for their capacity either to produce things that others can consume or to consume things that others have produced. There are many reasons for this not least the fact that the economic system that prevails requires the constant creation of new needs and of new products to meet those needs. Economic prosperity seems to depend on it: that what would have been considered a luxury before, or would not have even been thought of, is now a necessity. The ascetical disciplines of fasting and almsgiving oblige us to think again about this way of valuing humanity just as they help us to develop the virtues needed to resist it.

Fasting

Over indulgence in food and drink is always possible and it is often easier to find excuses for it than to recognise it simply as temptation. If we give ourselves over to the culture of blaming and litigation, of complaining and standing on one's rights, we run the risk of losing a sense of being blessed, the awareness of creation as a gift from a gracious God. A proper appreciation of the good things of the earth must include recognising where they come from, discerning how they are to be wisely used and remembering that there are other people in this world whose basic needs (food, water, shelter) are not being met while we are satisfying imaginary needs. Fasting cannot be simply a personal challenge to see if we can meet certain spiritual targets, a visit to a kind of spiritual gymnasium. Modesty in our intake of food and drink, and even abstinence from them, supports concentration and meditation, reminds us of the needs of others, and helps us to acknowledge the gifts of God.

John Paul II reminded consecrated religious of their need to rediscover the ascetical practices typical of the spiritual tradition of the Church. These are powerful aids to authentic progress in holiness, he said, helping to master and correct the inclinations of human nature wounded by sin, indispensable if we are to remain faithful and follow Jesus on the way of the cross (*Vita Consecrata* §38).

When Jesus speaks of almsgiving he warns against doing it in a way that draws attention to ourselves. The temptation of what is delightful to the eyes is not just about physical beauty that might arouse our lust but about how we want to appear to others, how we wish to be seen. It is about power and autonomy, being influential and recognisable, being in a position to help others and make them indebted to us. There are great dangers here and the virtues we need to resist them are those associated with justice: gratitude, respect, humility, truthfulness, generosity, as well as justice itself. We give alms to others not only by giving them a handout but also by respecting their property, by honouring their good name and reputation, by seeking to be honest in regard to their gifts and failings (as well as our own). In a world obsessed with fame and celebrity, with how people seem rather than how they are, there is more need than ever for followers of Jesus to be humble, comparing themselves only with God and thereby recognising their nothingness as well as their greatness.

The desire to count for something, to find one's place in the sun, even to have authority over others, can be as powerful as the desire for food or drink or sex. Who can survive being praised, the Book of Proverbs wonders (27:21). Who can stand up to riches, the Book of Sirach asks (31:10; see 1 *Tm* 6:10). There is nothing to be done except to engage in the combat these desires force on us. We must get involved in this combat if we are to remain directed towards our goal, if we are to continue to grow in the life Jesus gives us.

Prayer

If fasting seeks to manage the lust of the flesh and almsgiving the lust of the eyes, we can think of prayer as the Christian antidote to the pride of life. The original sin of pride is the decision to go it alone and to seek wisdom apart from God. To pray is to acknowledge our need of God. Another tendency of our time is to regard independence and autonomy as simply good, dependence and neediness as simply bad. But our situation is one of dependence and neediness: on parents and teachers, family and nation, friends and colleagues. Secular humanism fears that God is a threat to humanity, that we cannot be truly free until we shake off God. Adam and Eve, in seeking to be wise apart from God, are the original secularists. Christian humanism knows that the truth is directly contrary to this: Christ, who is the head of humanity, leads it not towards destruction but towards flourishing. Prayer is the fresh air in which the Christian lives and blossoms.

To submit our life to God in prayer is neither humiliating nor cowardly: it is simply truthful and spiritually healthy. To give up on prayer is to enter a place of loneliness and sadness. To persevere in the struggle of prayer requires courage but is the way saints are made.

Another Three: Poverty, Chastity, Obedience

Another act of the virtue of religion is the taking of vows and it will not come as a surprise to suggest that the three vows of religion may also be aligned with the threefold structure of temptation and the threefold asceticism of fasting, almsgiving and prayer. The vow of chastity seeks to manage the lust of the flesh, to order the fulfilment of physical desires, and to counter the deep-rooted tendency that leads us to focus on self to the exclusion of others and God. Poverty seeks to manage the lust of the eyes, to order our desire for cutting a dash and making an impression, and to counter the tendency to find our sense of identity in what we own or in what we manage to achieve. Obedience seeks to manage the pride of life, to order our involvement in God's plan in a way that is according to His will and not our own, and to counter the tendency to go it alone, to fall back on our own plans for our life and so miss the depth of what God's love has in mind for us. The names of these vows are also names of virtues that ought to characterise the lives of all Christians in ways appropriate to their relationships and commitments. Anyone who follows Christ must be poor, chaste and obedient. In publicly making profession of these vows, religious thus become a witness and sign to the Church as a whole of its own deepest reality and calling.

The Usefulness of Temptation

In the Bible temptation most often refers to a testing of the human heart by God. According to the Book of Proverbs

> the crucible is for silver, and the furnace is for gold, and the Lord tries hearts (17:3; see also 3:12; 27:21).

The Book of Sirach says

> My son, if you come forward to serve the Lord, prepare yourself for temptation. Set your heart right and be steadfast, and do not be hasty in time of calamity (2:1).

God weighs human hearts and tests them to see what they are made of (*Ps* 7:9; *Jr* 12:3; 1 *Th* 2:4). Why would God do this? In order, it seems, to purify our hearts so that we can love with greater integrity; in order also, it seems, to make human hearts grow bigger so that we can love more. God tests people in order to refine them: *Jr* 6:27; 9:7; *Zc* 13:9; *Ps* 66:10; *Is* 48:10; 1 *P* 1:7; *Ws* 3:5; *Sr* 2:5.

Temptation is then a necessary part of life with God, something potentially useful and helpful to us. St Luke points out that it was the Holy Spirit who led Jesus into the wilderness to be tempted/tested by the devil. The First Letter of Peter says we are not to be surprised at the 'fiery ordeal' that tests us as if something strange were happening to us (1 *P* 4:12; see 1 *Co* 10:13). God tests individuals (2 *Ch* 32:31; 2 *Co* 9:13) or the entire people (*Ex* 16:4; *Dt* 8:2, 16; *Jg* 2:22) often using the nations and other instruments (*Dt* 13:3; *Jg* 3:1,4; *Jdt* 8:25; *Ps* 11:5).

Temptation helps us to know what we really stand for. Only by facing options and making decisions do we come to know what it is we really value and where our hearts are really given. The struggle with temptation brings about a growth in self-knowledge. We learn about our weaknesses and blind spots, about the depth of our commitments and about the extent to which we are ready to serve God. In practice it is only through temptation that we come to distinguish what we really value from what we think we value. The struggle with temptation helps to clarify this difference for us.

It is easy to be virtuous when we have no choice. Faced with the choices that temptation offers we can, by choosing wisely and well, grow in virtue. St Teresa of Avila says that love is seen, not if it is kept hidden in corners but in the midst of the occasions of falling. Temptation then helps us to set our hearts right and to purify our loving by giving ourselves clearly and decisively to what is of real value.

Temptation usually involves struggle and difficulty, perhaps even blood, sweat and tears, but through such suffering we grow. Rather than shrinking us by limiting our options, our survival of temptation helps us to become greater and bigger than we were. The experience of struggling with it will mean that we will not be hasty in time of temptation but will grow in that calm wisdom which is a hallmark of holiness. Temptation hones the spirit and moral character of the human being:

> Blessed is any one who endures temptation. Such a one has stood the test and will receive the crown of life that the Lord has promised to those who love him (*Jm* 1:12; see also 1:3).

Temptation is, therefore, useful although the outcome of our struggle is not guaranteed. The value of the temptations of Jesus for us is in the knowledge that what we go through, he has gone through already. And as we go through it we have his help, strength and life to support us. The ascetical practices of fasting, almsgiving and prayer already strengthen us in virtue and prepare us for temptation. In Lent we turn our minds to the testing and training that Christian life requires but Lent serves simply to recall us to things that ought to mark our life always: honestly facing up to what it is we really value, and growing (even with some pain) in the faith and love of the Lord.

In his *Spiritual Combat*, Scupoli identifies four 'most sure and necessary weapons' in the spiritual warfare against self

- distrust of oneself
- trust in God
- spiritual exercises
- prayer.

Distrust of self and trust in God is an attitude quickly noted and discussed by him (chapters 2-6) but fundamental to his spiritual teaching. Thinking about the weakness of our nature in the face of temptation is already sufficient to encourage us to distrust self and trust God. When we recall that our struggle is with more than flesh and blood we are encouraged even further in this direction. It is to this aspect of spiritual warfare that we now turn.

Not Just Flesh
and Blood

Cosmic Battle

In the first chapter we proposed a triangular model for the spiritual struggle: temptation has three aspects (lust of the flesh, lust of the eyes, pride of life), there is a triangle in which we must live (relating to self, others, God), the classical works of asceticism are three (fasting, almsgiving, prayer), and the vows of religion, seeking to confront directly the threefold root of sin in us, are also three (chastity, poverty, obedience). But our struggle, as St Paul says in the Letter to the Ephesians, is not just with flesh and blood 'but against the principalities, against the powers, against the world rulers of this present darkness, against the spiritual hosts of wickedness in the heavenly places' (*Ep* 6:12). This is why the Christian, if he or she is to remain standing in the evil day, must 'put on the whole armour of God in order to stand against the wiles of the devil' (*Ep* 6:11,13).

There is any number of New Testament texts that speak about these spiritual hosts and about the struggle with them in which we are also involved. We do not have to turn to the Book of Revelation for the gospels themselves are full of this cosmic drama. In his ministry Jesus is not only a teacher and a healer, he is also an exorcist come to take on and to overpower the spirits of evil and sin, of sickness and death. The demons themselves recognise him as one more powerful than themselves. Reading through the narratives of the passion in all four gospels it is clear that things are happening not just on the level of the relationship between Jesus, the Father and ourselves, and not just on the political level of conflict and misunderstanding between Jesus, the Jewish leaders and the Romans, but intertwined with those, spiritual warfare in another sense is under way, a conflict between the kingdom of this world and the kingdom of God, involving realities that are beyond human beings but that are of crucial importance for us.

St Luke concludes his account of the temptations of Jesus by telling us that the devil departed from him 'until an opportune time' (*Lk* 4:13). That opportune time, the 'hour' of which Jesus often speaks, is the time of his passion, death and resurrection. The hour of Jesus is the hour of the paschal mystery through which we are redeemed. At the beginning of the account of Jesus washing the disciples' feet St John tells us that 'the devil had already put it into the heart of Judas Iscariot to betray him' (*Jn* 13:2). The time has come for the showdown. As it unfolds, it seems that darkness is triumphant and the prince of darkness has conquered yet again. Jesus is condemned, is crucified and dies on the cross. But God's power reaches even into the kingdom of death, the last enemy of humankind (1 *Co* 15:26), and the swallowing up of Jesus by death becomes the hour of the triumph of God's glory. The Father's only Son, freely accepting his death and having dwelt among the dead, is raised by the Father's power in the glory of the resurrection. His victory means new and eternal life for us.

The Invisible Creation

Whenever we say the Creed we express our faith in God as Creator of heaven and earth, and 'maker of all things visible and invisible'. How are we to understand this reference to the invisible creation? It means things invisible in themselves, not just invisible in the sense of not yet having come within our line of vision. Past or future events on this earth are invisible in that sense - we cannot witness them - but we know that the Creed means something more than this. It refers to immaterial creatures, made by God but spiritual and not physical. In the great hymn to Christ in the Letter to the Colossians we read that 'all things were created in him, through him and for him, in heaven and on earth, visible and invisible, whether thrones or dominions or principalities or authorities' (*Col* 1:16). The hymn is worth quoting in full and repays constant meditation:

God has delivered us from the dominion of darkness and transferred us to the kingdom of his beloved Son, in whom we have redemption, the forgiveness of sins.

> He is the image of the invisible God
> The firstborn of all creation
> For in him all things were created
> In heaven and on earth
> Visible and invisible
> Whether thrones or dominions
> Or principalities or authorities -
> All things were created through him and for him.
> He is before all things
> And in him all things hold together
> He is the head of the body, the church.
> He is the beginning, the firstborn from the dead, that in everything he might be pre-eminent. For in him all the fullness of God was pleased to dwell, and through him to reconcile to himself all things, whether on earth or in heaven, making peace by the blood of his cross (*Col* 1:13-20).

Notice that another point is quickly made, not only that there is an invisible creation but that, however we think of it, it does not fall outside the work of Christ. Christ is the firstborn of creation and everything that is created, whether visible or invisible, is created in him, through him and for him. Likewise Christ is the firstborn from the dead, the beginning of the new creation. In making peace by the blood of his cross he has reconciled all things to himself, not only things on earth but also things in heaven.

So we are not tempted to be Manichees. Manicheism is a recurring error that finds it easier to understand spiritual warfare - the battle between flesh and spirit, between evil and good - as a battle between two equal and opposing principles, the God who created the spiritual realm and another god who created the physical realm. St Augustine was persuaded by this view for a time until he came to see that evil too must fall within the plan and power of God. It is a more difficult teaching to understand, that the devil and his angels are creatures of God and not powers opposed to him on the same level as God. The powers of darkness, just as they do not fall outside God's creating power, do not fall outside the work of God's redemption in Christ, at least in the sense that they do not succeed in foiling that redemption. We are told that all things are made subject to Christ, all principalities and powers, even death itself, so that he can present an eternal kingdom to the Father when God will be all in all (1 *Co* 15:28; *Ep* 1:23). Evil does not have the last word and nor does sin or death.

Sin is Behovely

Julian of Norwich (1342-c.1420) tells us that Jesus revealed to her this strange fact, that 'sin is behovely'. It means sin is fitting and appropriate, even in some sense necessary. It does not mean that sin is nothing: think of the suffering it causes, Julian says. But 'sin is behovely' because God can make it serve His purposes. Paradoxically, those things that soil the glory of God are made to testify to that glory and mean it is more gloriously revealed. The liturgy of the Easter vigil puts it this way:

> O happy fault, O necessary sin of Adam, which gained for us so great a redeemer! [The original Latin says more: *O certe necessarium Adae peccatum, quod Christi morte deletum est! O felix culpa, quae talem ac tantum meruit habere Redemptorem!* O certainly necessary sin of Adam, which is cancelled by the death of Christ. O happy fault which gained such and so great a Redeemer.]

A contemporary theologian who has written much about this mystery of the victory of Christ over sin and evil is Hans Urs von Balthasar (1905-1988). Basing himself not only on texts of the New Testament such as the hymn in Colossians 1, but also on the experiences of Christian mystics, including his friend Adrienne von Speyr, Balthasar believes Christians are obliged to hope for the salvation of all. We cannot claim to know either that all are saved or that some are lost for the judgement belongs to God. But the commandment to love all obliges us to hope for the salvation of all. The moment in the paschal mystery that illustrates the truth of this doctrine is the descent of Christ into hell. What does it mean to say that 'he descended into Hell'? It means that the victory of Jesus reaches all corners of creation, even the darkest ones. There is no created place, time or experience that has not been touched by His redeeming power.

Angels and Demons

Our minds naturally ask the question 'what kinds of being are we talking about when we speak of spiritual creatures whether good or bad'. Some might be tempted to avoid the issue by saying that this way of thinking belongs to a cosmology we have outgrown (an underworld, a world and an overworld) and that the powers and principalities Jesus tackled are better explained in psychological, sociological or other terms.

After all, people often talk about struggling with their 'inner demons' and we know they are talking about psychological and moral battles. People talk about the power of invisible things like 'the market' or 'institutionalised prejudice' or 'the atmosphere in the group', realities that are in themselves invisible but whose effects and consequences are all too visible. There are impersonal things that are powerful in our world, though the Church has difficulty in accepting that there can be social sins in the strict sense whose evil is not attributable to individual human moral agents. But Christianity has always believed also in the reality of spiritual beings active within creation for good and for ill, in ways that are relevant to us and to our relationship with God.

A moment's reflection on our personal experiences of struggle in trying to live the Christian life will confirm that we are up against forces stronger than ourselves. Scupoli is in no doubt that the devil is active in trying to prevent and confuse our efforts to follow Christ more faithfully (*Spiritual Combat* chapters 16, 23, 27-32). John Paul II speaks of the 'diabolical deceit' that causes some evils to present themselves under the appearance of good (*Vita consecrata* §38). The devil uses things, people and events against us but only because God allows him to test us (*Rv* 2:10).

Nevertheless, St Paul expresses concern that the tempter might try us too hard (1 *Th* 3:5) and Jesus teaches us to pray that we not be led into temptation (*Mt* 6:13).

The Jesuit theologian Karl Rahner (1904-1984), writing about a 'theology of sleep', speaks about the supernatural battles that take place over the beds of sleeping Christians. Things happen in the course of the night. The Bible speaks of God revealing things in dreams. God's people are then more vulnerable to spiritual interference, a fact that is recognised in the liturgy of Compline, the prayer that seeks God's protection from the dangers of the night.

But even when awake we may be conscious of the interference and distraction of spiritual powers that are in us but not of us. In his Letter to the Romans St Paul makes the startling statement, 'I do not understand my own actions' (7:15). 'I do not do what I want', he continues, 'but do the very thing I hate. I can will what is right but I cannot do it. For I do not do the good I want, but the evil I do not want is what I do. Now if I do what I do not want, it is no longer I that do it, but sin which dwells within me' (*Rm* 7:15,18-20). This is very re-assuring, at least in helping us understand the reality of our struggle. In the story of Adam and Eve it is likewise re-assuring that there we see the presence and hear the voice of the tempter. In the same moment in which we are presented with human responsibility for evil we seem to be relieved of full responsibility for it. There are other forces at work around us and within us.

This is how wise teachers have always understood the spiritual struggle. The Bible itself tells us two things about sin. On the one hand it is free and conscious human action for which individual moral agents are responsible (*Ezk* 14:12-23; 18; *Jr* 31:29-30). On the other hand it is a power reaching beyond human capacities and leading us to actions that we do not fully understand (*Gn* 4:7; *Ex* 20:5; *Dt* 5:9). 'From hidden faults acquit me', Psalm 19 says. How can they be faults if they are hidden and how can they be hidden if they are faults?

Sin is a power working through us for which we cannot be asked to bear full responsibility. Although we strengthen the power of sin by our choices and actions, sin itself is more powerful than us, something in which we are unavoidably caught up. This has always been part of the Church's doctrine of original sin: we find ourselves in a situation not of our own making which nevertheless means we are alienated from God.

Scupoli anticipates modern psychology in speaking of things human beings do 'unconsciously' or as a result of what we might call (although he does not use this phrase) a 'death instinct' (*Spiritual Combat* chapters 12-15). There is something self-destructive and self-subversive in human beings, that leads us to act against our own best interests. Much of the spiritual struggle is with this 'death instinct' and as such it is a fight for our survival as spiritual beings and as believers. St Paul says it is sin dwelling within us. St Peter puts it more dramatically:

> Be sober, be watchful. Your adversary the devil prowls around like a roaring lion, seeking someone to devour. Resist him, firm in your faith (1 P 5:8-9).

Just as there are evil spirits whose influence we need to resist, so there are good spirits whose power helps us. There are good invisible powers and forces, like the spirit of a community that is charitable and truthful, or the atmosphere of prayer that attaches to places where holy lives have been led. Such realities also work on us and through us even though they are not things for which we can claim credit. Such good spirits are strengthened by our choices and actions although they too are more powerful than us.

The Church teaches us about the great Archangels Gabriel, Raphael and Michael, messengers of God sent to enlighten, guide and protect human beings. If we really believe in God's interest in all the details of our lives - 'every hair on your head has been counted' (*Mt* 10:29-30) - then the Church's teaching about guardian angels makes perfect sense: the heavenly world is as near to us as we are to ourselves and God's care supports us at all times. 'Turn but a stone and start a wing' is how the Catholic poet Francis Thompson expressed his faith in the closeness of the spiritual to the physical world. In another poem he says that Jacob's ladder, with its angelic traffic ascending and descending (*Gn* 28:12; *Jn* 1:51), is set up in every ordinary place, pitched as he puts it 'betwixt Heaven and Charing Cross'.

For his part, Thomas Merton (1915-1968), writes that the monk

> ...has his face turned toward the desert. His ears are attuned not to the echoes of the apostolate that storms the city of Babylon but to the silence of the far mountains on which the armies of God and the enemy confront one another in a mysterious battle, of which the battle in the world is only a pale reflection (*The Silent Life*, page 11).

Revelation 12 speaks about the great sign of a woman who has given birth to the one who is to rule the nations. With a great battle in progress around her, and the devil out to get her, she (Mary, the Church) is led to a refuge in the wilderness where she will be nourished.

Reflecting on this text, Merton says that 'the Monastic Church' hides her face in the mystery of the divine silence and prays while the great battle is being fought between earth and heaven. 'Her flight is not an evasion,' he says, for 'if the monk were able to understand what goes on inside him, he would be able to say how well he knows that the battle is being fought in his own heart' (pages 11-12). What is true of the monk is true of any Christian who seeks to follow Christ. It is not an evasion of responsibility to say we must contend with powers that are more than flesh and blood. It is, once again, simply to recognise the reality of our situation. The moral and spiritual struggle of the individual Christian is his way of participating in the great battle.

The Church exercises a ministry of exorcism not only in the simple exorcisms performed on every person who seeks to become a Christian but in the solemn exorcisms where demonic influence is judged to be at work. Apart from the human and other created spirits, though, whether the latter are good or evil, there is first and foremost the Holy Spirit who bears witness with our spirit that we are children of God (*Rm* 8:16). On what better ground can we stand in facing the threat of created spiritual powers than that established in us by the Uncreated Spirit, God Himself, poured into our hearts to make us partakers of the divine nature (*Rm* 5:5; 2 *P* 1:4).

Wrestling with God

We struggle, then, with flesh and blood, the temptations that come the way of everyone, the desire of the flesh, the desire of the eyes, and the pride of life. We struggle also with principalities and powers, 'the world rulers of this present darkness', those parts of the invisible creation that are against us. Always at our side, though, is the Lord, the God of Israel, a mighty warrior ready to fight. Jeremiah remained confident in his difficulties because he believed that the Lord, a dread warrior, was with him (*Jr* 20:11). In speaking about the gentle servant of the Lord, Isaiah speaks also about the strength of the Lord who supports him. The Lord is a mighty rock, he says, who holds his servant like an arrow in his quiver (*Is* 44:8; 49:2).

God is a warrior who undoes warriors (*Jr* 46:6,12). In the prophetic writings that speak about 'the great and terrible day of the Lord', God is presented as a warrior who strikes fear in the hearts of warriors but makes the poor feel as if they have become warriors (*Jl* 3:10; *Zp* 1:14). Zephaniah gives us one of the most memorable portraits of the warrior-God:

> The Lord, your God, is in your midst, a warrior who gives victory; he will rejoice over you with

gladness, he will renew you in his love; he will exult over you with loud singing as on a day of festival (*Zp* 3:17).

God fights always, though, for God's purposes and these do not necessarily coincide with particular purposes his people may decide for themselves from time to time. If God is the warrior-friend of a needy Israel, he is just as often the warrior-opponent of an arrogant and sinful Israel. In response to the sins of the people God can rise up against them, waking as from sleep, like a warrior shouting because of wine (*Ps* 78:65). God is majestic and fearful in his battle-array (*Jr* 50:42), impatiently crushing the loins of the unmerciful (*Sir* 35:22). Isaiah speaks of God going forth like a soldier, 'like a warrior he stirs up his fury, crying out, shouting aloud and showing himself mighty against his foes' (*Is* 42:13). The same God whose servant will not break a bruised reed or quench a dimly burning wick, will extinguish the armies of Babylon and 'quench them like a wick' (*Is* 43:17).

The Lord is a jealous God we are told time and again. God is fierce and uncompromising in both His justice and His love. The way in which God fights on our behalf is not, as we shall see, easily understood. Indeed it can seem, at times, as if God is actually fighting against our purposes. This is why we find ourselves struggling also with God, struggling to understand the mystery of God's love and the wisdom of what God is doing with our lives.

The Warrior God: For Us or Against Us?

The first place in the Bible where God is described as a warrior is Exodus 15. We sing it dramatically at the Easter Vigil: 'the Lord is a warrior, the Lord is his name' (*Ex* 15:3). In freeing the Hebrew slaves from Egypt, the Lord is ruthless in undoing the power of the Egyptians and wonderfully attentive to the needs of the people he calls his own. On the one hand are the fearful plagues and God's indifference to the fate of the Egyptians when the returning waters swamp their armies (*Ws* 18). On the other hand is God's tender care for the Hebrews. 'It was a night of watching by the Lord', we read in Exodus 12:42, a verse that the composer Felix Mendelssohn combined with a verse from Psalm 121 to give us that beautiful piece of music, 'he watching over Israel slumbers not nor sleeps'. The Book of Wisdom, in speaking about the warrior God, moves from tenderness to uncompromising strength in terms that anticipate the poetry of John Milton and the paintings of William Blake:

> For while gentle silence enveloped all things, and night in its swift course was now half gone, your all-powerful word leapt from heaven, from the

royal throne, into the midst of the land that was doomed, a stern warrior carrying the sharp sword of your authentic command, and stood and filled all things with death, and touched heaven while standing on the earth (*Ws* 18:14-16).

If God's indifference to the Egyptians is troubling, the conquest of Canaan that marked the arrival of the Hebrews into the Promised Land makes for troubling reading also. The Lord oversees the strategy and the battles involved in this conquest and genocide. A Christian, however, reading about the execution of the king of Ai, an execution carried out in fulfilment of the Lord's command, will inevitably think of another king who also ended his life hanging on a tree:

Joshua hanged the king of Ai on a tree until evening; and at sunset, Joshua commanded, and they took his body down from the tree, threw it down at the entrance of the gate of the city, and raised over it a great heap of stones (*Jos* 8.29).

From the perspective of the New Testament, looking back, this strange fact becomes clear, that there came a moment later when the Lord, the God of Israel, was himself treated as the enemy of his people. He became a curse and was nailed to a tree, despised and rejected by the ones he came to save.

If God is a warrior fighting on behalf of his people, the Hebrews, the agenda or project for which God is fighting, is not simply the political and territorial agenda and project of that people. Take the strange tale of Joshua meeting a man near Jericho on the eve of a battle. This man stood before him with a drawn sword in his hand. Joshua asked him, 'are you one of us or one of our adversaries', to which the man replied, 'neither, but as commander of the army of the Lord I have now come'. Joshua fell on his face to the earth and worshipped (*Jos* 5:13-15). 'Neither' makes it clear that if God is at that moment fighting for Israel it is for some purpose of his own that he is fighting, a purpose that cannot simply be identified with the worldly interests of Israel.

God attacks Moses, Abraham and Job

Moses, not long after his initial intimacy with God at the burning bush, becomes the victim of what seems like attempted murder at the hands of God. We read about it in Exodus 4: 'at a place where they spent the night the Lord met him and tried to kill him'. His wife grabbed a flint, circumcised their son, touched Moses' feet with the still bloody foreskin, and said 'truly you are a bridegroom of blood to me', at which point the Lord left Moses alone (*Ex* 4:24-26). This same Lord had just revealed himself to Moses as the God of his ancestors, the God of Abraham, Isaac and Jacob, and we know that the self-inflicted violence of circumcision was in place in the religion of these ancestors as a sign of the covenant with the Lord. What are we being taught by this strange tale? We are taught that the God who calls men and women to serve Him is a God of holiness, as fierce and uncompromising in His justice as He is fierce and uncompromising in His love. We are taught that God is truly a God who lies hidden, whose mysterious reality is within the cloud of darkness into which Moses will eventually be led.

Moses and Abraham are the only two people whom the Bible describes as friends of God (*Ex* 33:11; *Jm* 2:23). This does not prevent Abraham being assaulted by God anymore than it spared Moses. (There is a story of St Teresa of Avila complaining to Jesus about how he was treating her. On being told by him that this was how he treated his friends she is said to have replied 'then it is no wonder you have so few'.) In Abraham's case the attempt is not on his own life but on that of his son (*Gn* 22). God tests Abraham and even uses him as His instrument in this strange sacrifice. For Judaism and Islam as well as for Christianity, this test of Abraham's faith is the supreme moment in his relationship with God. The trust he showed then, trusting God even when He asked him to kill the heir of the promise, makes him 'our father in faith', as the Roman Canon puts it. Once again, though, a Christian hearing that God spared the son of Abraham will inevitably think of the fact that 'God did not spare his own Son but gave him up for us all' (*Rm* 8:32). For later Jewish tradition, God's sending of the Messiah is a reward for the faith shown by Abraham. The Book of Judith notes that Isaac is also tested in this event (8:26).

God allows Satan to test Job. Satan is here just another member of the heavenly court with a particular portfolio to administer (*Jb* 1:6-12) and Job himself is in no doubt that his real adversary is God. His friend, Eliphaz the Temanite, suggests that Job's difficulties arise because he has run stubbornly against God with a thick-bossed shield. On the contrary, says Job, the attack is in the other direction. 'My adversary sharpens his eyes against me', he says, 'and has gnashed his teeth at me. He set me up as his target, his archers surround me, he slashes open my kidneys and shows no mercy. He bursts upon me again and again, he rushes at me like a warrior' (*Jb* 16:9,12-14; see also *Ps* 39:10; 60:1ff).

Those who come forward to serve the Lord must prepare themselves for temptation, the Book of Sirach says, they must be ready to be put to the test (*Sir* 2:1). It was the Spirit that led Jesus (*Mt* 4:1; *Lk* 4:1-2), perhaps even drove him (*Mk* 1:12), into the wilderness to be tempted by the devil. Jesus can pray - and pray sincerely, as we believe - the opening words of Psalm 22, 'my God, my God, why have you forsaken me'. For, like Abraham, Moses and Job, Jesus seems to become the target of God's wrath:

> Why are you so far from helping me, from the words of my groaning? I cry by day but you do not answer; and by night, but find no rest. I am poured out like water, and all my bones are out of joint; my heart is like wax; it is melted within my breast; my mouth is dried up like a potsherd, and my tongue sticks to my jaws; you lay me in the dust of death. (But) to him shall all who sleep in the earth bow down; before him shall bow all who go down to the dust, and I shall live for him (*Ps* 22:1-2,14-15,29).

So we must be ready for moments in our lives when God will seem to contradict Himself, when He seems to have turned against us. Such moments are unlikely to be as dramatic as anything we read of in the Bible but they will still test us deeply, perhaps even to the core of our being. We are ready for it intellectually, perhaps, if we enjoy the work of studying and teaching philosophy and theology. We know that the living and true God finds ways to smash the idols that we set up, the conceptions and images of God that are all inadequate and that need to be constantly undone as we enter more deeply into the darkness of the mystery of God. But we must be ready for the same process of purification at other levels of our experience and involvements. In the practice of prayer, at the level of our feelings, in our relationships with others, in the successes and failures that come our way, in the struggle with sin - within all of this we must wrestle not only with flesh and blood, and not only with the spiritual hosts of wickedness, we must wrestle above all with God.

Victory or Defeat?

This is the most radical but the most fruitful spiritual warfare in which we are obliged to engage. St John of the Cross called this struggle with God 'the dark night of the soul'. One of the biblical stories on which it is most useful to meditate in regard to this dark night is the story of Jacob wrestling with God at the ford of the Jabbok (*Gn* 32). In reminding consecrated religious (and indeed all the followers of Jesus) that the path to holiness involves the acceptance of spiritual combat, John Paul II says that 'tradition has often seen an image of this spiritual combat in Jacob's wrestling with the mystery of God, whom he confronts in order to receive his blessing and to see him' (*Vita consecrata* §38).

The first thing we must say about it is that Jacob's wrestling was with God, not against God, but along with God, the two of them obliged, it seems, to engage with each other in the way they did for the purpose of Jacob's vocation and salvation. It was a struggle not to the death but to the life, a struggle through the night to the birth of a new man, born at daybreak, with a new name. His physical limping is trivial compared with the moral and spiritual stumbling that characterised his life before. The night that is the place of deception and lies, the place of ambivalence and uncertainty, the time for flight and evasion, is also the night of watching by the Lord, the night of waiting for the moment of birth, the holy night in which Christ is born and rises from the dead.

If we were to ask, in regard to the wrestling of Jacob, a question like the one Joshua asked of the man he met near Jericho, 'who won', the answer seems to be 'neither'. Jacob survives but limps. He has stood up to God but has been wounded in the intimacy of his person. The outcome is both a defeat and a victory. Jacob becomes Israel as a result of this encounter because in it he sees the face of God. The Book of Wisdom says of Jacob that 'in his arduous contest she (wisdom) gave him the victory, so that he might learn that godliness is more powerful than anything else' (*Ws* 10:12). Notice the way it is put: Jacob is given the victory so that he might learn. The prophet Hosea also speaks of it as both a victory and a surrender: 'In the womb he tried to supplant his brother and in his manhood he strove with God. He strove with the angel and prevailed, he wept and sought his favour' (*Hs* 12:3-4).

Job's struggle with God also concludes with a defeat that is an amazing victory. Initially reduced to silence by God's discourse, Job finally manages to reply directly to God. The most remarkable of the things he says is this: 'I had heard of you by the hearing of the ear but now my eye sees you' (*Jb* 42:5). Some new realisation or experience of God is the outcome of Job's long struggle. He does not receive an answer to his questions at the level at which he put them but is led instead to understand more deeply the mystery of God. Like Moses he is led into the dark cloud in which God is said to dwell. A Christian reading of Job will see it not simply as a philosophical discourse about the mystery of evil and suffering, but as a remarkable setting of the scene for the coming of Jesus who is God's final answer to Job's question.

If we wish to see God we must be prepared for this strange and wonderful combat. It was experienced by patriarchs and prophets of the Old Testament and continues to be experienced by apostles and saints of the New Testament. It was experienced supremely by Christ, defeated by the final darkness of death but rising in glory from among the dead, still bearing the wounds of the struggle which has definitively opened the doors for all who would see God.

In the homily at the Mass to inaugurate his ministry as Pope, Benedict XVI said:

> Are we not perhaps all afraid in some way? If we let Christ enter fully into our lives, if we open ourselves totally to him, are we not afraid that He might take something away from us? Are we not perhaps afraid to give up something significant, something unique, something that makes life so beautiful? Do we not then risk ending up diminished and deprived of our freedom? ... No! If we let Christ into our lives, we lose nothing, nothing, absolutely nothing of what makes life free, beautiful and great. No! Only in this friendship are the doors of life opened wide. Only in this friendship is the great potential of human existence truly revealed. Only in this friendship do we experience beauty and liberation. ... Do not be afraid of Christ! He takes nothing away, and he gives you everything. When we give ourselves to him, we receive a hundredfold in return. Yes, open, open wide the doors to Christ - and you will find true life (24 April 2005).

How is such opening wide of the doors to Christ done? In a poem called 'An Imperfect Sonnet', a contemporary Catholic poet (who prefers to remain anonymous but has given permission for his work to be used) may be speaking of this aspect of the spiritual struggle when he writes:

What shape a prison cell?
No light to tell.
What face a guarded fear?
Unknown yet near.
What price a long lost joy?
A happy boy.
What moment in his life
Foreshadowed strife?

The secret lurking in the depths
What way to take it in what net?
Allow the light to shine into the cell.
Allow the fear to show its face again.
Allow the boy to feel once more his joy.
Allow the strife break open to new life.

But how, allow?

Christ, Our Champion

If we have to contend with temptation, then so had Jesus. In his response to temptation he showed that he is the servant of the Lord, loving God with his whole heart and soul and mind. If we have to contend with powers and principalities that are more than flesh and blood, then so had Jesus. He is the strong man who has driven the demons out and ransacked their houses. He has taken on the prince of devils and disarmed him (*Lk* 11:22). If we, like Jacob, have to contend with God, 'wrestling along with God', then Jesus in Gethsemane and on Calvary has already so contended.

Or is he the one who is not required to contend in this way, with God, because he has come to us from the Father, because he and the Father are one (*Jn* 10:30)? Jacob called it Peniel, the place where he had seen God face to face. But St John tells us that no one has ever seen God and that it is the only Son who is in the bosom of the Father who has made him known (*Jn* 1:18). What *we* have seen, John says, is the glory of the only Son revealed on the cross (*Jn* 1:14). Because he is the Word of God, the One who knows and has seen, Jesus reveals the Father to us. As the sinless one his struggle is not exactly ours. Not that this removes him from us: rather does it heighten his sensitivity to the effects of sin and evil.

Jesus is Stripped of his Garments

What glory is there in that shameful death, what beauty to attract us? Humanly speaking the hour seems like defeat for Jesus and victory for the powers ranged against him. Here is no warrior God arrayed in his panoply, a heavily armoured God to terrify and intimidate. Instead of a mighty warrior smiting and smashing his enemies we see the Son of God powerless and defenceless, like a sheep that before its shearers is dumb and like a lamb led to the slaughter (*Is* 53:7). He is abandoned and naked, exposed to whatever his enemies choose to do to him.

On that day, says the prophet Amos, the stout of heart among the mighty shall flee naked, a text that Mark may be alluding to when he tells us about a young man who runs off naked at the moment of Jesus' arrest (*Am* 2.16; *Mk* 14.51). We are told (unnecessarily it seems) that this young man was wearing only a linen cloth. But linen cloths have powerful associations in the scriptures. Half the references to linen in the Bible are found in those chapters of Exodus and Leviticus that describe the clothing of priests. All the references to underclothing in the *New Revised Standard Version* translation of the Bible are to the linen undergarments worn by priests who are not to come naked into the sanctuary. We are not told that the tunic of Jesus - his undergarment as the Jerusalem Bible translates it - was made of linen but we are told that it was seamless (a reference apparently to the seamless robe of the high priest: *Jerusalem Bible*, note to *Jn* 19:23).

Jesus is a priest through the power of an indestructible life and not through physical descent (*Heb* 7.16). His way was not to stand on his dignity but to empty himself, to take off the robe of his glory, to become a slave who washes the feet of his disciples, to allow himself to be stripped of his garments and nailed to the cross, entering the battle with nothing except his knowledge and love of the Father, entering the sanctuary with nothing except his own blood (*Ph* 2:6-7; *Jn* 13:4; *Heb* 9:12).

It was a naked David who faced Goliath and triumphed. Saul wanted him to wear his armour but David, trying it on, could not move. So he stripped himself of it, took five stones from the river and with just one killed the Philistine champion. Jesus stripped naked and marked with five wounds looks like the defeated one but, just as he has the power to lay down his life, so he has the power to take it up again (*Jn* 10:18).

The prophet Isaiah, in one of those strange acts required of prophets, walked naked and barefoot for three years as a sign and a portent against Egypt and Ethiopia (*Is* 20:2-3). Whether Egypt and Ethiopia were impressed by this threat we are not told but it alerts us to another kind of power. The sword of the Word of God exposes all, judges the secret emotions and thoughts, no created thing can hide from him, everything is uncovered and open to the eyes of the one to whom we must give account of ourselves (*Heb* 4:12-13). Jesus, we are told, did not trust himself to them, never needed evidence about any man and could tell what a man had in him (*Jn* 2.24-25). He is the Word that penetrates to the heart, that probes the loins.

Our champion, then, is naked, vulnerable and powerless, and yet he prevails. Armed only with his knowledge and love of the Father, Jesus stands against the powers of this world and against the spiritual army of evil in the heavenly places. The campaign of Jesus takes him to crucifixion on Golgotha where he engages directly with the last enemy, death, and appears to suffer defeat. The devil has taken the bait, as some of the Fathers of the Church put it, not realising that hidden within is the double-edged sword, the divine Word, the devil's undoing because he is the father of lies and Jesus is the Word of truth.

The Anglo-Saxon poem, *The Dream of the Rood*, has the cross of Jesus speak as follows about the one it bears:

> The young hero stripped himself - he,
> God Almighty - Strong and stout-minded.
> He mounted high gallows,
> Bold before many, when he would loose mankind.
> I shook when that Man clasped me.
> I dared, still, not bow to earth,
> Fall to earth's fields, but had to stand fast.
> Rood was I reared. I lifted a mighty King,
> Lord of the heavens, dared not to bend.

In the seed that has been sown a new and glorious life is already germinating. So he goes to the spirits in prison to preach to them (1 *P* 3:19). He visits the kingdom of the dead. One of Job's friends reminded him that Hades and Abaddon had always been naked and uncovered to the sight of God (*Jb* 26:6) but that place is now touched by God's re-creating power. From among the dead Jesus rises in the glory of the resurrection to be given the name that is above all other names in heaven, on earth or under the earth (*Ph* 2:9-11).

The love and obedience of Jesus, revealed in his submission to death, are vindicated by his exaltation to the right hand of the Father. The place of abandonment and sorrow has become the place of reconciliation and glory. Jesus, the tested one, comes through (*Is* 28:16; 48:10; *Heb* 2:18; 4:15) so that the cross of the Lord has become the tree of life for us. And there is even greater good news in all this because the victory achieved by Christ on our behalf becomes, by his grace, our victory also. 'Thanks be to God, who gives us the victory through our Lord Jesus Christ' (1 *Co* 15:57). 'Those who prove victorious I will allow to share my throne, just as I was victorious myself and took my place with my Father on his throne' (*Rv* 3:21).

Prophet, Priest, King

If Christ is our champion, our leader and guide in the spiritual struggle, it is in the first place as our great high priest that he is this champion, the priest who is his own sacrificial offering. He is a priest like Melchisedech, the Letter to the Hebrews tells us, not through physical descent but by the power of an indestructible life (7:16). Our high priest has gone through to the highest heaven (4:14) and has entered the sanctuary once and for all, taking nothing with him but his own blood. By virtue of that one single offering he has won an eternal redemption (9:12) and achieved the eternal perfection of all whom he is sanctifying (10:14).

What makes his priesthood even more a matter of rejoicing for us is that he is one of us. The one who sanctifies and the ones who are sanctified are of the same stock (2:11). It was essential that he should become completely like us so that he could be a compassionate and trustworthy high priest of God's religion (2:17). We rejoice then that we do not have a high priest incapable of feeling our weaknesses, but one who has been tempted in every way that we are though he is without sin (4:15; 2:18). He is not only an example for us but also a source of grace and mercy reaching to our inner selves and changing our way of living. In offering himself as the perfect sacrifice to God through the eternal Spirit, Christ purifies our inner self from dead actions so that we do our service to the living God (9:14).

He is the leader who takes us to our salvation (2:10) but this leadership meant his identifying with us before we could be identified with him. He, before any of the rest of us, was made perfect through suffering (2:10) and, although he was Son, learnt to obey through suffering (5:8). During his life on earth he offered up prayer and entreaty, aloud and in silent tears, to the one who had the power to save him out of death, and he submitted so humbly that his prayer was heard (5:7). The reference is to his agony in Gethsemane, perhaps also to his desolation on the cross. There, above all, he submitted with such reverence, and was so obedient to the Father's will, that his prayer was heard. The Father's will was for us to be made holy by the offering of the body of Jesus Christ once and for all (10:10). His death takes away all the power of the devil and sets free all who had been held in slavery all their lives by the fear of death (2:14).

It follows that his power to save is utterly certain, since he is living forever to intercede for all who come to God through him (7:25). He is our judge, testing our work (1 *Co* 3:13), and this too is great good news. Who else would we want as the judge of our lives? And how can we now fear any spiritual warfare to which we are called when we have such a champion to intercede for us and to stand with us?

The Armour of Light

So we are to take our part in a struggle that is already in principle resolved. We have been delivered from the dominion of darkness and transferred to the kingdom of the beloved Son (*Col* 1:13) and yet we are to complete what is lacking in Christ's afflictions for the sake of his body the Church (*Col* 1:24). We are to lay aside the works of darkness and put on the armour of light (*Rm* 13:12). If we are to stand against the wiles of the devil we must put on the whole armour of God (*Ep* 6:11,13).

So how do we dress for this battle? What is our protection and weaponry? If we are following Christ and engaged in his battle then we will not put our trust in the impressive regalia of priests or the intimidating armour of soldiers. Ephesians 6 describes as follows the armour in which the Christian must dress for the spiritual warfare:

> ... stand your ground, with truth buckled round your waist, and integrity for a breast plate, wearing for shoes on your feet the eagerness to spread the gospel of peace and always carrying the shield of faith so that you can use it to put out the burning arrows of the evil one ... accept salvation from God to be your helmet and receive the word of God from the Spirit to use as a sword (*Ep* 6:14-17; see also 1 *Th* 5:8).

The armour which the Old Testament says is worn by God (*Is* 11:4-5; 59:16-18; *Ws* 5:17-23) is worn now also by Christians. The warrior God of the Old Testament has called to his side those who belong to Christ and in the power of their belonging to Christ they become participants in the battle and not just beneficiaries of its outcome. The sword that is the Word of God, alive and active, cutting more finely than any double-edged sword (*Heb* 4:12), is placed by the Spirit in the hands of the Christian (*Ep* 6:17). This is not about war in the ordinary sense. These weapons of truth, integrity, eagerness for the gospel, faith, salvation and the Word of God build a spiritual kingdom not an earthly one. The armies of heaven are clothed in fine linen which is the righteous deeds of the saints (*Rv* 19:8,14). The work of acquiring these virtues and gifts (insofar as their acquisition is within our control) is considered in the longest section of Scupoli's *Spiritual Combat* (chapters 7-43).

Spirituality False and True

The grace of Christ lifts us beyond natural spirituality and mysticism to a theological life. It is important to remember that there is a natural level of spirituality and mysticism that is not yet the deepest level on which the Christian lives. In writing about the years immediately preceding the conversion to Christianity of the Emperor Constantine, E.R. Dodds makes a helpful distinction between the daemonic and the divine worlds (*Pagan and Christian in an Age of Anxiety*, chapters 2 and 3). The first is the level on which much contemporary spirituality operates: religious experiences that can be generated from our own resources relating to what is often now called 'the divine'. In speaking of the human being's relation to the divine world Dodds means what Christians will refer to as the theological level, that level of 'experience beneath experience' where the theological gifts of faith, hope and charity are to be located (1 *Co* 13:13).

It is through these gifts (also called theological virtues) that we live already the life of the kingdom Christ has won for us. Through faith and the sacraments, especially the Eucharist, the cosmos is transformed and humanity transfigured. Through hope and prayer the ordinary Christian foot soldier is ready for the long road and can live with courage and perseverance. Through charity and the corporal works of mercy the one who follows Christ is living an ecstatic life, empowered by love to emerge from the shell of his ego to reach out to the neighbour in need.

The spiritual warfare in which we are involved may grow intense at times. Its forms will be myriad and confusing. Recalling the seven deadly sins is enough to remind us of the many ways in which we can be seduced and distracted, of the many fronts on which battle needs to be waged: pride, covetousness, lust, anger, gluttony, envy and sloth. Without Jesus we are naked and defenceless, as he was on the cross, easy meat for the devil, who is going around like a roaring lion looking for someone to eat. More than likely we will be wounded in these struggles, perhaps seriously, but we pray that those wounds will be rendered glorious and that through God's wonderful providence even our sins will be transformed to become witnesses to His grace.

The cross of the Lord is become the tree of life for us. The word of the cross is folly and scandal to those who do not believe but to those who do believe it is the trophy of victory. In the cross we see the wise strategy and indestructible power of God. This is how Paul puts it in his most famous passage about spiritual warfare:

Who shall separate us from the love of Christ? Shall tribulation, or distress, or persecution, or famine, or nakedness, or peril, or sword? No, in all these things we are more than conquerors through him who loved us. For I am sure that neither death, nor life, nor angels, nor principalities, nor things present, nor things to come, nor powers, nor height, nor depth, nor anything else in all creation, will be able to separate us from the love of God in Christ Jesus our Lord (*Rm* 8:35,37-39).

Further reading

Balthasar, Hans Urs von, *Dare We Hope That All Men Be Saved? With A Short Discourse on Hell* Ignatius Press, San Francisco, 1988

Dodds, E.R., *Pagan and Christian in an Age of Anxiety* Norton, London and New York, 1970

De Lubac, Henri, 'Spiritual Warfare', in *Theology in History* Ignatius Press, San Francisco, 1996, pages 488-501

Julian of Norwich, *Revelations of Divine Love* Penguin Classics, 1966

John Paul II, *Post-Synodal Apostolic Exhortation* Vita Consecrata *on the Consecrated Life and its Mission in the Church and in the World*, 1996, §38

Kauffmann, Jean-Paul, *Wrestling with the Angel: The Mystery of Delacroix's Mural* Vintage Books, London, 2004

McCurry, Jeffrey, 'Why the devil fell. A lesson in spiritual theology from Aquinas's *Summa Theologiae*' *New Blackfriars* 87 (2006) 380-95

Merton, Thomas, *The Silent Life* London, 1957

Rahner, Karl, 'A spiritual dialogue at evening: on sleep, prayer, and other subjects', in *Theological Investigations III* Helicon Press, Baltimore and DLT, London, 1967, pages 220-236

Robinson, Jonathan, *Spiritual Combat Revisited* Ignatius Press, San Francisco, 2003

Scupoli, Lorenzo, *The Spiritual Combat* Burns Oates and Washbourne, London, 1935

Christian Meaning of Time

For Christians, time is full of meaning, and through it God speaks to us in many ways. This booklet explores how the time of creation, the history of salvation in the Bible, the Church's year, and even the end of time as we know it, all speak to us of the love of God. Time is God's gift which allows us to draw closer to Him and our eternal destiny in heaven.

The *Deeper Christianity Series* delves into the mysteries of Christianity, opening up the spiritual treasures of the Church.

David Fagerberg teaches in the Department of Theology at the University of Notre Dame, USA. He has written on the topic of liturgical theology, has an avid interest in Chesterton and is author of The Size of Chesterton's Catholicism.

ISBN: 1 86082 392 0

CTS Code: SP 15

Deepening Prayer

Prayer is at the heart of the Christian life, but is always a battle. This booklet explores some of the major methods of Christian prayer, as well as the problems and pitfalls. Sr Mary David uses the wisdom of the Church Fathers to lead people of today into a deeper relationship with God.

The *Deeper Christianity Series* delves into the mysteries of Christianity, opening up the spiritual treasures of the Church.

Sr Mary David is a nun of the Benedictine community of St Cecilia's Abbey in Ryde on the Isle of Wight.

ISBN: 1 86082 382 3

CTS Code: SP 13

Union with God

St Athanasius famously said that "the Son of God became man so that we might become God". This booklet delves into what it means for a Christian not only to have a relationship with God but become so united with Him that we take part in his divinity.

The *Deeper Christianity Series* delves into the mysteries of Christianity, opening up the spiritual treasures of the Church.

Fr David Vincent Meconi, SJ is a member of the Chicago Province (USA) of the Society of Jesus. His academic speciality is the thought of St Augustine of Hippo and the place of prayer and the emergence of a Christian culture in the early Church.

ISBN: 1 86082 392 0

CTS Code: SP 12

Informative Catholic Reading

We hope that you have enjoyed reading this booklet.

If you would like to find out more about CTS booklets we'll send you our free information pack and catalogue.

Please send us your details:

Name ....

Address ....

....

....

Postcode ....

Telephone...

Email ....

Send to: CTS, 40-46 Harleyford Road,
                Vauxhall, London
                SE11 5AY

Tel: 020 7640 0042
Fax: 020 7640 0046
Email: info@cts-online.org.uk